MOUNTAINS ARE FOR CLIMBING

MOUNTAINS ARE FOR CLIMBING

by Letitia Gail Lowery

The Naylor Company
Book Publishers of the Southwest
San Antonio, Texas

To All My Friends

CONTENTS

PERSONAL

PREFACE

To begin this preface, I would like to express my deepest gratitude to those who have inspired me to write each of the poems included in *Mountains Are for Climbing*. . . . These people are the great number of boys and girls that I meet in my everyday life. They are my friends and loved ones. They have inspired me to put my feelings to poetry in a way that could not be expressed in any other way.

This book contains poetry consisting of everyday life, love, nature, religion and my very own personal poems. In each section you will find my feelings expressed in a way which one can understand better than any other type of expression which I have yet been able to accept.

Love,
Letitia Lowery
Age 17

LOVE

MISUNDERSTANDING

Love . . . who can understand
This wave in human nature?
It is a theme that lifts you up
As well as lets you fall
Into the ever-glowing pit of heartbreak.
What man is there
Who would cast love away
With an apathetic air,
Letting self rule the heart?
Let this man not be let
To live while in this gesture,
For love makes the world go round,
While in other cases, makes others end.

SONG OF LOVE

Love: hankering, beckoning and unruly assaulting,
There stands the side as dark as ebony.
Yet, then love, in its glory, laud, and honor
Beseeches us all into a mind-blowing coma.
Where is this glory? Is it the prime face
That stands gleaming in the dark doorway
That sometimes bestows flowers of beauty
Yet brings on thoughts of grapes of wrath?
Where is the laud? Do you honor a hope
That could verily send you to an early grave?
But Love comes brighter, yea, with the stars,
Beckons gleams of hope, that lift your eyes
Upward into the Heavens, upheaving dreams.
Love is the rustling run through the lone prairie
At earliest sunrise, browsing amidst the flowers
And at last, plucking the heartwarming rose.
But as one places this ruby to sip the smell
Ofttimes they caress sharp endearments
That draw blood, and ravage the senses.
One had just better be haughty of the
Handling of the rose, like as to love.
Love holds its peaceful extravaganzas
That mold into loving blissful futures
And bring, alas, soothing ever-afters
As well as prime-in-thought smiles.
Oh, persons, live for this ever-glowing solemnity
In the feat to bestow love to all mankind.
One can never know the flavor of the stream
Till one has sipped the rippling waters.
So, therefore, cast no love away, even
Though love seems to put you away
Even into a crevice of heartaches and tears

4

Which burn up what pride there still cleaves.
Calmly flow these subtle waters, until a stone
Is cast and creates a rippling splash. . . .
So goes with love, in the dueling realm of life
For Love is not solemn. Love is motile.
Love is the smile upon a damsel's face at sight
Of marital status. . . . Love is the gift of
Flowers to the elderly one's bosom.
Alas, Love is the gift of Eternal life
From our Heavenly Father which gave
All the love He withheld upon the giving
Of His beloved Son to die for our own true woes.
Woe should be upon us for His unacclaimed identity!
Some shout of love and joy when they
Have not yet met the Son of such force!
Is freedom so saturated with love?
Freedom cannot come from disbelief,
For belief is the basis of all gifts of God.
Two souls walk along in the dark o' the night;
Two souls walk along in the heat o' the day;
They caress hearts as they caress hands;
They walk along the Road of Life together;
Becoming drunk upon each other's tears
Yet, willing to swallow them and carry on.
They hold enough devotion to push aside the
Pride that could verily hurl them apart,
But through all hinges, the door is always open
To abundance and love, that makes forgiving,
As well as forgetting, the key to the
Everlasting happiness that can adorn
Even the poorest of paupers, or richest of royals. . . .

QUESTION OF APPROACH

Besiege me the words
To write a love poem.
I become speechless.
My mind grows blank.
I approach the introduction
And have loss of words.
I start to wonder
If love has lost rank.

Maybe it's just that
Love's been crammed down my throat
In so many awesome ways.
I have to admit this:
Maybe I don't understand love,
Or the kind that stays.

Surely I've found such
In one of my meetings
With youth or truth
To befall. . . .
Could I see thru
Blinds of heartbreak
That maybe I haven't yet met
Real love at all?

LOVE'S SILENT VENTURE

Silence broke thru the night.
A window creaked, then
There was hushed silence.
Tho' night's candles burned low
No sound was heard.
Even of night-cloaked violence.
Down the riverside, all uptight
They hovered to tiptoe
To the hidden black lake.
They wiped away dew from their brow
And continued to walk, till
They met, greetings to partake.
Night's candles, burned out
Seemed to echo in the night
And broke silent calm.
They unclasped each one's hearts,
They must surely part,
But no, hardness was come. . . .
Love does the good evil,
And evil good.
The sayer is only chastised
And the doer is understood.

MORE THAN SUNSHINE

More than sunshine
Does the rainbow come.
More than liking
Is the truly beloved.
In case of the heartbreaker,
The time of no gladness.
Instead is the heartbreak.
Instead is the sadness.
Can you really tell
To whom they belong?
To the liker? The beloved?
Which one is the wrong?

ARRANGEMENT

That which you loved that's gone
Is forgettable,
But that which you loved that still loves you
Is unforgettable.
Can you forget one that has his picture
Permanently planted in your mind's eye?

SCARRED

Can you bury grand memories to
Make up for the bad ones showing through?
A blessing sweet; a haunt, sour?
What then comes to the mind?
Sometimes the mind seems to waver,
To halt, to rest, to pray.
Therefore, is the heart so afflicted
That it, too, touches and wounds the soul?
Wounds so deep that they hurt physically
As well as mentally . . .
Yet who can heal a wound that is so
Deep that a scar is promised?
Who takes away the scar?
The person who puts it there. . . .

HOW DO YOU MEND ONE?

Who hasn't loved could never know
Just how I feel.
I feel like a sunken ship, a wounded dove;
How then else can you describe a broken heart?
But not only does the broken heart
Tear the brain, rag the soul,
Kill the will, but then how do you
Mend one?

SIGHTS

My eyes
do not
burn still
searching
for old
tranquility,
for your
love is
beautiful
to see. . . .

THE JOKER

Laughter had been the utmost cause
To make the sun rise for him each day.
His sublime joy within life was to
Make a joke of others, and to gape
With laughter at his own hurting whelms.
Even tho' his gestures made his smile
This pain hurt the ones he loved
And the ones who tried to love him.
They had swallowed each spear he had thrown
But to this day the blades had sharpened,
Then, alas, one day his sun did not rise.
Yet, like a boomerang, his sword turned
For it had pierced the heart of one he loved,
And then it surely was not laughter
That was running down his cheeks.

THIEF IN THE NIGHT

Darkness is
Where the heart is,
Because love is
A multitude of shadows.
Love comes like
A thief in the night,
And when you decide
All is alright
Dawn breaks,
And you find that
It has robbed you.

14

UNDECIDED ONE

There walks this youth,
Bubbling over with answers
Like as to a fountain, yet
He does not heed them.
Instead, mixed-up, walks he
Just in a gaze upon
The unjust green earth
Not knowing where
To head, who to speak to,
What to turn to,
Who to turn to,
Where to go, or
Who to love. . . .
Could it be that
Rigid disastrous time
Has made this one
Wonder why to love?

LOVE IS

Translucent dreams
Cannot revile
The aim of seeking
For a smile.
Some want to show
Their undying love
In ways so opposite
Of that above,
And instead of listening
They love to send
Gifts and favors,
No heart to lend.
They place Pride on top
And even so
They think that money
Is the way to go.
But tho' money sends
Dreams come true,
Still, love is the
Little things you do.

TO REMEMBER

Amidst the four prime seasons
Autumn walked in, surrounded by hearts.
Autumn was friendly, and had more
To smile about. . . .
The Autumn leaves were so beautiful,
So full of life and gaiety
That they were kept in a scrapbook
Of memories, of this degree of love.
The book was shoved far back
Into the cold gray closets of the mind,
And then snow began to fall.
It fell, heavily, beginning to bury
All remains of this Red Autumn.
And for a while, it was as if Old
Autumn had never shown its red face
To the world, for life was a
Gloaming of white . . . but as
The scrapbook was brought from the
Darkness, it was recalled
And the snow began to melt.

REMEMBRANCE

That Everlasting Autumn
Brought my soul to the
Realization of how much
Worth is a home.
The cooling winds opened
My eyes, once closed,
To realize there are others,
To cease my roam.
Yea, though I feel no
Hunger pains or sweat
Anymore, the Anticipating
Winter sometimes bestows
Letdown, and though I
Dare not, an Autumn leaf
Alights, oftentimes
When the wind blows. . . .

I LOVE YOU

I love you . . .
Because you have brought me a garden,
A garden of springtime and seasons
That bloom to a beautiful scent.
I love you . . .
Because you were the sunshine of summer,
A summer of silk sand and warm nights
That helped you to know what I meant
— When I said I loved you . . .

BROWN EYES

Brown eyes . . .
Cast your chestnut
Blooms upon my
Green eyes, ripe
With an unbounding
Love that reaches
For you in slumber
And in wake. . . .
True eyes . . .
Cast your welcomed glance
Upon my blushing face
Soft, with an uneasy
Care that watches you
For my sake. . . .
My love, the beauty,
Deep within your eyes' spark
Is a painting of the love
Beautiful, within your heart.

20

THIS GUY

This guy . . .
Is he the reason why
I feel the gentle way
I do?
This guy . . .
Is he the reason why
I love the skies of
Gentle blue?
If he . . .
Could move a mountain
It would be the
Same as changing me,
But now . . .
I have a clear mind
Of the way I've
Turned out to be.
. . . And I can see
Beyond the sea!
This guy . . .
Must be the reason why
I feel the gentle way
I do . . .

WHO SAID?

Who said he knew love?
Who has got the right,
To lend his own fortunes
To loving and light?
Who said he found love?
Is he right or wrong?
The answer, true answer,
Is there in his song.
Who said he lost love?
Who cast out the fears
And lost all his loving
In a warm stream of tears?
Who said he cursed love,
And said love was cruel?
Who is to say now
That he is a fool?

C-O-M-E

Come fly away with me, my love,
For we're playing the same tune.
I have to take you along, my love,
So said the velvet Moon. . . .
For the Moon shadows that have
Long followed my every step
Cast a lovely glow on you, my love,
Whom all my love has kept. . . .
So ride the climbing sky with me!
Come lend me your sweet hand,
And love me just because I'm me,
And together we shall stand. . . .

LOVING REST

Swing low, my heart,
And cherish his caress.
The love God sent
Has made it here and
God is there to bless.
Bend low, my dear,
And let me taste the wine,
And if I cannot touch you,
I'll wonder if you're mine.
Kneel low, my knees,
And thank my soulful God.
He lulled my heart to rest
And caused my head to nod.

SO LOVED

I vow to give to my utmost plea
Beaucoups of love I've found in me,
To show my respect and thankful heart
I've given to my love right from the start.

I long to promise sweet dreams forever,
And think of the days my love will not sever.
So precious he is, and forever will be,
A part of my soul, so loved by me . . .

MY LOVE IS SOFT

My love is soft —
Soft touch, soft smile,
Dark laughing eyes,
And tender style.
My love is calm —
Calm stare, calm mind,
An assuring clasp
To love's tight bind.
My love is sure —
Sure speech, sure hand,
Sure blushing eyes
That take their stand.
My love is rare —
Rare boy, rare sweet,
And the most wonderful
Person I've yet to meet.

I SPEAK OF LOVE, VERILY

I speak of love, verily,
When I speak of
Treasured surroundings;
Evening, cool, and morning, dim.
I partake in love, sharingly,
When I place my steps
Into the silver crystaled dew;
The breezes, cool, upon my face
And moisture, soft, upon my skin.
I look at love, merrily,
When the first glare of sun
Rises, red, above the sleepy dawn,
And the glow settles, light, upon the hair
Of my love, sweet of Heaven's kin. . . .

NATURE

SUNDOWN

Sundown . . . your beauty just surrounded me.
Sundown . . . I found the ruby glaze in you.
Sundown . . . though the sky is baby blue,
I'll still find my golden days deeply in you.
Sunrise . . . you blessed the fields with gold.
Sunrise . . . you made my eyes no longer blind.
Sunrise . . . you woke the ebony which was night
And made the stars hide from your spotlight.

BEAUTIFUL

What is beautiful?
Beautiful is the morning, dew-pearled by the twilight mist.
Beautiful is the sunlight
Left mingling with the dawn upon the high hills and ridged
    land.
Beautiful is the seashore
Touched with morning's blessing of natural sunlight and
    sand
Which curls the tangled waves,
And salt which seems to delight in lying upon the rocks and
    rills.
Beautiful is the happiness,
And the happiness that any person will find if and when he
    will step
Into the morning, with the day
And smile at the sun, rain, heavy hardships as well as joy
And when a storm brews
Cast it away and admit surely that it was beautiful . . .

SILVER

All God's supreme and immortal blessings
Come down upon a flow in a realm of light.
It blesses brooks, blesses the green earth,
Even making this color easier to see.
Oh, come to see a young maiden within a walk
Along the country green.
She has no thought of happiness,
But only the hope that is unseen.
She wipes her brow from sweat and tears
That cause her stride to falter.
Oh, lend your hand, God, to your child
Oh, try and quench your daughter.
Here comes the immortal blessing, then,
God sends His own to transform pain.
I sometimes hasten to curse this rain,
But somewhere on the earth, someone
Is praying for it . . .
I look not to my own selfish whelms
All the time, for someone on the
Earth was praying for it . . .

TOO LATE, THE SUN

I did not know that God's own beauty
Was polished by the rain. . . .
I should've wept for my own selfishness
Who cursed this shower of blessing.
I hear the thanks of the toads,
And the gratitude of the swine.
I sense the glow of all the creation
As this silver fills the streets.
Up high in the evening peaks
I see the ol' lazy sun who has
Finally begun to show his brow.
Yet, too late the sun has come,
For its bedtime is nigh. . . .
The stars shove the sun aside
For their own appearance. . . .
Lazy, sun, who did not wake up this
Grey day . . . Lazy sun, so lazy,
Who must've slept through all the rain.

DELIGHT IN YOUR OWN BEING

What is jealousy,
And where is perseverance
Thru this doting mood?
I look, and ask because
I confront this whelm
In such different focuses
Of my constant days.
I face jealousy at eye's
Length and longing but
I know this is wrong.
A person is only who
He will be, and will
Not be changed unless
He is a traitor to his
Own personality. How else
Face I jealousy? From
The eyes that seek
At my own being and
Wish they were me . . .
Jealousy has no friend.
It loses them daily.
One should not resort to such;
Delight in your own being.

JOURNEY

Musically
The crystaled waters
Slithered and skidded
Upon
The snow-white stones,
Slowly
Lapping and lining
The damp banks,
Silently
Journeying to the arms
Of the velvet blue sea.

SO GLOWS HOPE

Golden sunshine, gleaming, glimmering,
Never ceases to cast
Its warm and fresh glow
Upon those whose hopes
Are righteous dreams
And the uneasiest
To sever. . . .
The stormy clouds, brewing,
Looking hungrily from the
Jeweled and fluent sky
Seek out the illusioned,
And will cast a shadow
Upon the hopeless forsaken
Forever . . .

BLUE JAY ON A RAINY DAY

The blue jay lights
Upon the crystaled leaves.
It hops about, being
Colored by the rain.
Soon it will be once
More flying . . . flying
In the gray sky.
Tho' for a scare, if I
Were the bird, I, too,
Would stay upon the ground,
Only until the gray goes
Away . . . And the sky
Would be my greatest
Refuge. . . .

SILVER BLESSINGS

Golden fingers
Slithered thru
The darkened morsels
Of atmosphere
And absorbed the
Silver which filled
The streets.
Pulling it,
Grasp by grasp
Back into Heaven
To be blessed
Upon other frontiers.
The gold fireball,
Embarrassed, cold,
Slid behind the clouds,
As once more,
Nonchalantly, softly,
Silver streams
Blanketed the sky.
. . . made green the land.
. . . made damp the sand.
. . . made thankful the Man.

EVERYDAY LIFE

HOME

You may as well go on home.
You're left out all alone.
You could have been halfhearted in your
Attempt to get fully stoned.
You've lived out in the cold.
Your life is light and bold.
Why not go home . . . or maybe find one?
Come on and see the sky.
There's a twinkle in your eye,
And everywhere you go, you see a sun of ruby red.
I guess you're going to play
Out there in the hay,
Why not go home . . . or maybe find one?
Living is just a will
That makes your heart be still
And sometimes you may cry when you think you've
Lost your sigh,
But you may as well go home.
You can't make it all alone. . . .
Why not go home . . . or maybe find one?

LOOK UPON

Look upon any morning dew
And you may find a will
To leave the common range. . . .
Look upon any seeking of personal needs
And you may lift your roots
To resort to the land of strange.
However be the sight of heart,
If age be your only foe,
You will find in youth, perseverance
That cannot battle true woe.

AID

Though cry as you may
It seldom calms fears.
Much swells the heart
On cravence of tears.
You cry o'er lost love,
But what has been lost?
A buddy, a pal?
Who'll count the cost?
For some black time now
I've forgotten how to smile,
And let tears be my motto,
And heartache, my guile.
Until I met reason
I roved with the wind.
You calm fear with endurance
And Heavenly amends. . . .

45

WHAT IS SIXTEEN?

I don't know exactly
How long this note will be.
I only know I aim to
Open up some eyes to see.
It's really hard
To live a life today
When all you hear is,
"Please, kid, stay away."
It's sometimes hard to stay a good Christian,
When all you hear is sinful and so wrong.
It's only life we have but to encounter,
And all is well till sweet love comes along.
Love comes with drums,
And brings pretty balloons
Dances in on hearts,
And forecasts full moons.
A lover's sighing heart
Is seldom blue,
When you are young,
And your lover is young, too.
You're full of life so you just want to sing out.
You want to fling out and have your very own song.
How can you keep everyone else happy?
Who is your boss? To whom do you belong?
You laugh out loud now.
You're unafraid to cry.
You kiss away teardrops.
You pray into the sky.
Why are your feelings
So hard to hold in hand?

You want to laugh at folks
Who say they understand!
Poor child of woe, Lord!
They're undelighted!
They're undecided!
They're just united!
They cannot hasten dreams.
They're only "just" a teen.
So goes the meaning
Of the world.
I have decided
I'll grow on up someday,
But I dread it,
Because I'll treat others this way
That I've been treated,
But, yet, I vow I'll treat them kind.
They need understanding
To bring them peace of mind.
What is sixteen?
Is it eternal bliss?
Is it the 140th kiss?
The time some seem to miss?
What is sixteen?
Is it knowing right from wrong?
Who can tell them how,
When they each have their own song?
What is sixteen?
Though I hate to say the words;
It's being old enough to speak out,
But still too young to be heard. . . .

COME FORTH

Silence broken is silence turned loss.
Memories outspoken are thoughts to toss.
All that used to be grows forth with age,
And the child is to be let out of the cage.

The child is to be let out into the realm of life,
Knowing that failure can surely bring strife.
Be this the motion of pure lover's will,
And shall the child wait till all is still?

Is this age that could calm the force?
That could make aloud your heart's course?
One can only know how one can smile
And heart knows if it can wait a while.

Let the child come forth and act his age.
Unlock the key; suffer the child from the cage!

THE SEASHORE HOLDS THE STORY

The seashore holds
The story of all
That have ever
Walked upon its sand.
The seashore is memories,
Memories of past fate
Yet the seashore is always
There, and always will be.
However, the tide also
Wipes prints in the sand
Away when it laps the shore.
Now the memory is not
A reality, yet a dream,
And the sea will hold
Firm dreams forever.

IN ONE WORLD

The sun shines hot upon our heads.
We live under the same sun.
The stars brighten the dark of the night.
The stars, the same to everyone.
Tears fall, making memories realities.
Tears, not of the same gland.
However, when tragedy inflicts pain,
Tears are the answer of each man.

SOMETIMES

Sometimes a person
Feels as if they are
As downtrodden as the
Grass . . . being walked upon,
And the color is gone,
And before long,
The person is gone. . . .

GROWING UP

No longer can the play
Change, alas, within the mood.
No longer can the role of life
Have changes understood.
So long was reality play,
Shadowed by imagination.
Life has come to be no act,
No solitaire or degradation.
These childlike whelms that used
To be, have surely run their course.
For now, instead of acting love,
We begin to know the source.
One cannot haste to adulthood.
Childhood dreams are uneasy to sever.
Childhood was only a mere way of saying,
"On a clear day you can see forever."

HOPE UPON THE LAND

The Sea of Life, though roughly flows,
Is guided only by hope, the
Ship misguided, may be great loss.
Only God leads the safe sail.
The safe sail is as if storms
Had ne'er brewed o'er the sea
Yet tiny storms still erupt
And make you doubt, although
Your Sea of Life cannot always
Be silent, transformed with love,
Far above the storm rides
Calm as music, the dove of hope.

BASKETBALL GAME

. . . and the Crowd, becoming
As solemn as grass, lost one
Precious breath in the praise of
Ten of their town's own.
The seconds passed far too
Fastly; The scare was on,
And people seemed to be sweating
Pure precious blood.
The crowd, the onlookers, clasped
All the inner hope they possessed
Into the triumphant screams, and
Shock, never getting out of hand
For fear of costly disapproval.
Such a war to be fought, with
No casualties, except for the
Defeated . . . and the defeated
Are the ones who will know
How dark and cold the war was.
The crowd arose, as in worship
And with shrieks of jubilance
Lifted their ten own boys
High into the air, for they,
Once more, were the Undefeated.

54

THERE ARE TIMES WITHIN LIFE

There are times within life
That you wish you had
Never breathed upon the earth,
That you had never shed your
First tear, for this crimson deed
Began a life of tears.
There are valleys within life
That seem too deep to attempt
For fear of coldness beneath it;
The act of cold letdown.
There are rivers within life
That seem too deep to wade
Yet too shallow to sail.
There are seas within life
That seem too stormy to
Cross over; the problems are
Multiplying, and engulf you.
There are heartbreaks within life
That you wish you'd never had.
There are times within life
That you wish you'd never cared.

WILD GOOSE CHASE

Walk down the hallway
That leads to a marbled room
Containing peace for all mankind.
And when you have reached
This treasured surrounding
Do not lose the key, alike to our
Forefathers, leaving us to lie
In the dark, as they once were,
Striving to find the right doorway,
Constantly making our way
In the dark . . . searching.
Searching, like blind babes
Or mute objects, who have no
Clue as to where their destination is,
And half the time, forgetting
What their destination was. . . .

STEP IN!

Come as you will . . .
. . . Come as you are!
Fasten your dreams to
An oncoming star!
Look to the front;
Bury your past!
Let your future find you,
And it will be fast!
Did you murmur "love"?
Did you murmur "care"?
Step into your future,
. . . and they will be there.

A SONG IS IN THE MAKING

A Song is in the making,
Of what has not been sung.
A cry is the partaking
Of a new and crucial wrong.
A song is for the joyful
Who cherish dark and light.
A song is for the noble
Who make the wrong be right.

CORNERED

Cornered into
A laughing span,
Is the daily zoo,
The growth of Man.

RELIGION

SEA OF EVERLASTING TEMPTATION

Lo, night after night, I just pray, Lord,
That you will find for me a way.
I hasten to keep out of barrings
That marrow my Christian soul away.
I long to follow Thy footsteps.
I'm beside Thee all the way,
But human fouls make me stumble
And fall into the whey.
The whey is sin, O almighty source!
The longing I sought for redemption
Sometimes looks narrow and coarse.
But faith, I know can jolt the mountains,
And faith, I know, can direct my course.
Lord, upon the Sea of Life, direct my sail
And guide me safely o'er the stormy peaks,
For the savage waters of sin only rock
And slowly my ship does take the leaks.
But Thy hand, a deliveress, leads me on
Caressing my last bit of life inside.
And I'll follow on o'er the stormy sea
Hanging to Thy coattail, I ride. . . .

TWO HUNDRED MILLION

Two hundred million
Cried for peace
Of almighty World War II,
And two hundred million
Died in wars
To let live me and you.
Two hundred million
Roved the streets
In cries of human rights.
Two hundred million
Broke our peace,
Burned the land, to fight.
Two hundred million
Laughed at God.
They said that he was dead.
Two hundred million
Beheld Christ's descent.
Too late, they bowed their heads.

HELPING HAND, ALWAYS THERE

Tho' imaginary discomforts befall me,
And send my soul no release,
I look to my Heavenly Father
For inner hope and peace.
This peace I find in knowing
That he will always care.
This hope is his bestowing
That he'll always be there.
God will lend his hand of mercy,
Whatever be your pardoned sin,
If you'll look up to Heaven
And ask Him to come in. . . .

REQUEST

Oft heard's the swear
"There is no God,"
And many say tis so,
Yet some of these
What came they from?
The sea or mid air?
What made them grow?
What began this claim?
A group of God's own
Who had no feelings
But of Almighty Self?
But look upon the
Rising and falling tides.
Without the sun, to
What is it cleft?
Man, you can mechanize
Your own knowledge and power,
But I ask to see
A Man make a flower. . . .

THREE GIFTS

What gift have I
If I have not Christ
To show my encore?
What peace have I
If I have not will
For mankind to implore?
And what hope have I
If I have not strength
To knock upon God's door?
Door of hope; opening to peace:
Here will I find true release
From my ill-planned life,
From the fingers of strife.
Christ, my will, and strength,
Will determine my life's length.

GOD, THANK YOU!

God, thank you for wings
I would not have known
To fly from this world
Of contagion and night.
God, thank you for things
Like kindness and love,
Like Your Son that You gave
To help us see light.
God, thank You for Hope
That mingles with time
And glides with the fortune
That gladness can bring,
Like the Sun of Tomorrow
Ascending with peace
And the joy that had brought
My lost heart to sing!

FREE

I'm free — let it be shouted
To the ears of a lonely crowd!
I'll live — and I'll be happy,
And I'll die and still be proud.
Christ came and saved me
From my weary rest.
Love came and made me
No longer alone.
Still I am free, free to
Go as I please,
Knowing He, and His
Love led me home. . . .

YOU WERE LEFT BEHIND

The stars all have fallen
Deep within the sea.
The sky is not the color
That it used to be.
The moon is no longer
A pale yellow glow
But a mass of blood,
Dark and hallow.
The seas have touched
The shores their last
And red is the stain
That buries their past.
Along with the changes
From out of the sky
Came a rapture and a tumult
Of a trumpet's shrill cry.
Billowed on clouds
The Lord came back down,
While people gasped
And scurried around.
Then all at once
The Dead turned to life
And grasped hands with the living
Who would not have strife.
Thousands ascended
With eyes to the sky
And you were left behind;
Too late to wonder why.

Too late to wonder why
The stars fell down upon you.
Too late to grasp the hand
Of the Son so living True.
Tho' flames of wrath engulf you,
You'll always keep in mind
When the Saved of God ascended
And YOU were left behind. . . .

I WISH

I'd like to make a start
In the heart of a soul
Who's reaching for a hand.
I'd like to wish a will
For the pill he's taking
To help him live on the land.
My wish for him who's breaking,
Partaking and making
A sad life more complete,
Would be to lift your eyes
To God, and him to meet.

JESUS SAID

People screeched
like a train
and bled
like the rain.
People laughed
at the dying
and scoffed
at the crying.
People ran
from creation
and buried
a nation.
People stood
high on sin
having no
heart within.
People said
God was dead,
and cursed
His homestead.
People hid
from the bombing.
Jesus said,
"I am coming!"

GOD'S BOMB

From far away,
On a hill, I stood,
All tearful, with
My eyes to the sky,
And watched the sun
Caress the morning dew
And smiled at God's
Creation and so did cry.
I cried just to know
That within that silky air
Was a cloud of hate
So strong, not bland.
And then I knew
That the only sad creation
Was the bomb that God
Created called Man. . . .

NEXT IS COME

Hopeful peace
Has passed
Beyond the horizon.
The last of peace has come.
Only now
The second
Phase of Life is nigh,
For next is come The Son.

PERSONAL

BEING FREE

Being free is being able to pick your
Own mountain and climb it by yourself.
Being free is being light as a feather
And just blowing in the breeze.
Being free is still smiling
When You need to shed some tears.
Being free is mounting up your voices
Into one feeling of ease.
Being free is having a care about the world
Like you want everybody else to see.
Being free is being able to love
With no doubt who it should be.
Being free is surveying your own dreams
With a fragment of severing hopes;
Being free is the unbounding radiance
That God sends ne'er to grope.
Being free is being me.

MY SONG

Slipping and sliding into angry deep
And the love at the bottom is my cravence.
Running and hiding in the valleys steep,
Run and find my own heart's cravence.
I like to think that the trees are all
Put there for my eyes to behold.
I like to think that my treasure is peace
Which cannot be found in silver or gold.
I like to swing upon the smiles of life,
And glide about with the unruly wind,
For the simple fact is, the sky is my home,
And the sea is my refreshening.
If you like the smell of air, soft,
Then you might want to ride my train with me.
It's all your life. I could share it,
But you must like to swim in the breeze.
For you might find the water a blessing
And come join my cry of peace.
And if so, then I will tell you once again,
That my prime destiny in life is to win.

PARDON ME

Pardon me if my little crimson
Hopes do not delight you,
But the simple fact is that
What I think roves with the wind.
Pardon me if my hopes do less
Than could ever right you,
Because my hopes are my own to win.
Pardon me if I look like a person
Who has the wrong-way street,
But the simple truth is, it is my life!
If my pardoning does not unite us,
Then I guess there's no sense to fight.
There's no sense to shower me with
Angry words, for they will only raise my will.
There's no sense to touch me in anger deep
For it makes my thoughts deeper within.
Pardon me if what I do does not delight you.
Pardon you, for it does not concern you!

IT TAKES A LOT

It takes a lot to understand me,
To see thru my slum moods,
And upheaving smiles.
It takes a lot to mend my woes, and
Wipe away my tears and rough
Beguiles.
I sometimes think I rove with moods,
And no one else can calm my day.
But then is when my love walks in,
And then my world is pleasant as May.
It takes a lot to see my smile,
And truly know the reason it's free.
I sometimes think that thru my life,
It takes a lot sometimes to love me.

ACCOUNT OF WILL

. . . And I look to the almighty wind
Of comfort when I have need to
Look for consolation from the
Weariness of this ill-planned life.

And only at certain times does
This ill-kept wind heed my longings
And lend a helping hand to the
Soul of my being.

And at this holy, blessed
Age of perseverance, and only at
This time, do I feel fully committed
To the wind of
My own delightful solitude.

NINETEEN SEVENTY-ONE

I do believe, that in this
Oppressive year I have
Met life face-to-face
And upon many idealized meetings
I have overlooked my cause.
So, surely do all youth
Have reflections in their overbearing
Teen years to look back upon,
Think about, and glare upon,
And say, "How did I ever do this?"
But in those times, whate'er they be,
They are the recipes for memory,
Memory that can give one a time
To look back upon a lesson learned
Or experience that was daring.
These memories in early age
One can also be thankful for,
If after these buried mistakes
It dies, before time to come
Could mar a lifetime. . . .

TELEGRAM

Boy, hurry back, running,
Caress, and take heed.
You are my destiny.
I crave you as need.
I've been troubled
With outgoers,
Though fulfilled with pride,
They tempt me, constrain me;
I don't take them in stride.
Instead, I wait for you
And hold feelings inside.
You are the sunshine
My spirit does ride.
If my holdback is hopeless,
If I need not wait,
Much glows if you'd tell me,
For this I do state:
O'er all this tumult
Your face is above.
Above all my constrainments
I send all my love . . .

NEW SONG

Alas, I journeyed outside
My olden keepings
Of the iron-barred gates
And heeded to stay out.
My soul tended to
Falter, and heave loneliness.
I buried rooted chastisement
Yet one still holds the scars
Of accidents in the Sea of Life.
So living was a destiny
Of heart and soul, combined,
And when love once lost is
Love profaned, I will to
Forget that first meeting.
Yet a scar still cleaves
Until one of similar abundance
Makes it fade, fade away.
So I met one, and felt belonged,
And closely ceased chastisement,
And created a new song. . . .

THE REALIZATION

I cried into the night
For no one would befriend me.
I walked the lonesome road
To seek a helping hand.
Can no one lift his head
To see sorrow in my face?
Can no one lend a touch
To help me take my stand?
I take my stand, alas,
Upon my own two feet.
Within my private mind
Memories fade away. . . .
I should've known all along
That until I faced myself,
And lived up to my will
I'd never find the way.

DESTINY

Sometimes, even at my early age,
I feel as if I've ventured thru
All the hardships of life
Just trying to find myself.
Some days I feel as if I
Have found myself, then all
My happiness seems to seep thru
A hidden crevice to my fears.
What is that strife that
Seems to befall me?
That seems to put me on the
Track, as well as let me fall?
I ask, because I grow afraid.
Afraid of the cold world . . .
Yet brave, with God on my side,
And Pride as my weapon.

NO RUNNING AWAY

I, a person, at times feel the need
To resort to mind, to heed.
The pain I feel can only be felt
By the supreme being that's dealt.
Tis best to merely trust yourself;
Tho' may cut your pride, tarnish your wealth.
But all in all, upon the pardoned end,
God will take care of his children.
In life, we learn, we live, and love.
This right is sprung from High Above.
And when night is dark and dark is day,
We sometimes want to run away.
But whatever the reason, beware the claim.
Your pains will spring upon you and gain.
They'll gain in measure, worse than before,
Which will make you sad, make you sore.
Trust this word, for this word is true.
Heed to this fact, whatever you do.
You cannot run away from reality.
Take it from experience. Take it from me.

THE TIME HAS COME

The time has come; the time has brought us here.
We have no chance; our chances cast on fear.
Our love has grown, more than the days gone past.
How can we say which day will be our last?
We sob on woe; oh, woeful are our woes.
How can we live? Our parents are our foes!
We cannot see each other comfortably.
Our feelings still stay hid, but outward all can see
The close stares, blinks of love that glow from us.
The hurting pain is going to suffer us!
Oh, hail, what's next? Another problem here?
We cannot see, for we, to each, are too dear?
There is no way to hide a broken heart,
But can we kill a love that's grown from the start?
God's will is clear. . . . He says it plainly,
That we may have hope, but then mainly,
He bids us split, but what of broken hearts?
Look to the bad? Forget the better parts?

PART OF THIS GLOAMING

As I lie crouched upon my stomach against grass
I moresoever feel part of God's gloaming.
I lie, all limbs outstretched upon the ground.
My long hair sways in the wind, like any
Leaf on any shrub blowing in the field.
My body, with a semi-film of sand stands
Alike to the coated bushes and grasses
Blown onto by dust's sheen.
Cool breezes make my soul seem to shiver,
Though the weather is humid and dry.
At once I feel my blood begin to boil,
And wholly laugh at the tho't of it!
Who now belongs under Man's shelter,
Destined to work under Man's rule?
Who now belongs to not sleep on his own time,
Eat when he wishes, laugh when he does please?
I say no, for I feel like I belong in this satisfying nature.
I have not the time to feel all alone,
I'm too much on fire for God's perfect beauty.
The more I pave my path through this valley
The more I love this palace of wilderness.
If being so, hence, I pray that I live upon this
Pleasant and peaceful gloaming thru all the days
I have yet to live upon this Earth. . . .
If I'm to live here, cannot I be free?
When I die, cannot I die, only to leave
My bones to rattle in the wind here?

CRY

I don't really care if he's wealthy.
I just want him to have a heart.
He doesn't have to be a sex symbol or anything
But good looks do count, if you ask me.
I hope he's not the type who won't call me,
And he'll never leave me hanging from a ledge.
I want him to come over often,
I mean, practically, live at my house, you know.
Mainly I want him to stand by me, love me as I love him.
That's always been the trouble with boys I've liked.
They just kept leading me on!
But they won't anymore, I grant you!
I'm just as fragile as any female,
And just as apt to love and hurt.

PREDICTION

Stand ready, my lagging heart.
Soon you shall meet another.
Are you not desperate for
Someone you could trust?
Someone who could not
Weaken you?
Poor dear heart . . . you're worn
To a frazzle!
But look with a healthy prediction
Toward the future,
When another heart shall comfort
You, I hope, pray, and aim!
Dear heart, I promise you this —
— His heart will mend your broken one.

DEFEAT

I've always thought of myself as
Lucky — a winner, a celebrity,
Looking at males who cast their eyes
And never doubting a one.
Spoiled . . . that word describes me,
But then where do I stand now?
A rose in a bed of thorns?
A flower surrounded by weeds?
My heart's weak; it must be by now.
So many males have trampled upon it,
Tearing it. . . . What's left to a life
Where the only one you're living for
You may as well forget?
What is "forget"? Somehow that word
Haunts me now for it wasn't until now
That it occurred to me as my only way out,
My only answer . . . my only degree!
I, the winner, the celebrity, stand defeated,
Defeated, as it may seem . . . and
Lo, I cry at the thought of it.

UNREALITY

Upon certain feelings, tides
Of shock and buoyant hopes
I feel as light and as free-going
As the wind . . . too thin
To see, and too swift to touch.
My mind, blowing like a breeze,
Brings my feelings to seem
As if I am floating,
Floating, upon a soft mellow
Cloud. . . . Everything is smooth
And has a glossy surface.
Care? What is care . . . for
Maybe I am content or even
A blob of nerves just now
Sliding off the road, the
Dark road of loneliness into
A fulfilling valley of dreams.
Light and care goes the wind.
Light and unreal go I.
Unbelievable, I take a step
Into the cool gloaming of unreality
And memory, if not but one
Time in my ill-planned life.

THE JOKER IS WILD

I try to talk to him.
I sound serious; I am serious,
Yet he makes of my seriousness
Indeed a joke, and laughs.
I used to think he'd be the
One who could lift me out
Of my olden woes. . . . But
How can you depend on one
Who makes fun of your
Every action and just
Walks away? Truly, I
Am getting tired of chasing
Him down, trying to make
Him listen to my seriousness,
For when I speak with
An air of love, he acts as if
I have just told a good joke.
So, from now on, I'm silent as the
Dew, acting as if I don't care,
Waiting for the time when
He will . . .

I, A THINKER

I walk down a
Long stretch of land.
Just thinking, and
Memories haunt me.
I think of present
Ideals, but then the
Present is a letdown.
The present is black,
With cold loneliness;
The past is red,
With heartbreak;
And the future is blue
With doubt.
God, why was I
Born a thinker?
Being a thinker
Makes me sometimes
Wonder why I
Was even born. . . .

ALL AT ONCE

All at once my utmost
Childhood realities appear
And I am once more
Running through the world, so clear.
I pause aside the languid waters,
And pluck a bloom from the green.
The sky is nothing less than
Cotton on blue, the stars, an open screen.
Life, so carefree, is a jolting swing.
The action lowers, then up again.
My only pains are life displayed
In playing "Grown-up." So goes the wind.
My dreams are those of fairy tales.
I laugh at solemn tears.
Carefree was I, to laugh at woe,
A change wrought through the years!

ALAS ALONE

I walked alone, as always
Down the afternoon lane.
His stares of hope were assurance.
He cared, and all was plain!
I even smiled at dust today
As it caressed my stride.
A whelm inside me made me sing.
This whelm, my glee did ride.
I kicked a stone into a stream.
It splashed and I did laugh
At just the thought he DID love me;
Loneliness was no longer my staff.
I sat beside the cooling tide
And my heart sensed to moan.
I shouldn't have decided to think
For alas, I still feel alone.
Suddenly blueness o'ertook me
And the dust burned my eyes.
Was the dust what made tears fall?
Or was it his new-laid lies?

HOME

City streets
And morning towns
Led me to
Search around
And the gaslights
Made me feel
I was alone.
But the country
And the green
Woke my soul
To better things,
And the sun that
Winked its eye
Said I was home!

MY WORLD

My world is sunshine,
Sprinkled with rain,
Misty mornings
And evening sand.
My world is glory,
Sheltered by smiles,
Laughing eyes
And reaching hand.
My world is starglo,
Glistened by night,
Pale sad moons
And frosty dew.
My world is tranquil,
Thirsty with need,
Loving seasons
And wanting You.

WAKENED

This is MY beautiful world!
I have conquered the day!
I have sprung from slumber
With great expectations
And eyes heavy with tears.
I have come from the sod,
Sod of the earth to be free,
And thank God, free I am!
I have conquered the day!
This is God's beautiful world.

I WONDER

I wondered what I thought to win!
I wondered who could seal my smile.
I wondered when I'd learn to cry.
I wondered when I'd gain beguile.
I wonder what I saw in him —
I wonder who could end my crave —
I wonder when he'll leave me be —
I wonder why the love I gave. . . .

BURIAL NOTE

God came and took me from my weary day,
And when I did you thought that I had died,
But really I just ventured too high into the sky,
Now is there really any reason why you cried?
God knows best, so why waste the tears?
He never makes mistakes so it was worth the years.
God wanted me here or he would not have reached
To the Earth, found me, and brought me up.
Surely lovers cry . . . hey, who is crying for me?
Bend low, bow your head, and say good-bye.
I mean, we knew it would happen someday,
And God always knows when the time is right.
So even though I would still love to be with you,
Live, be happy and full of delight.
Be fruitful, in what I left behind me to remember.
Be remembering my good times, sad and gay.
Think of me as only a crumb of life that blew away.
Dream of me and I will see you again someday.
Remember me as a person who smiled at the sun.
Remember me as one who believed in crying.
Remember me as one who was unafraid to live,
And even more unafraid of dying . . .